Horses Picture Book

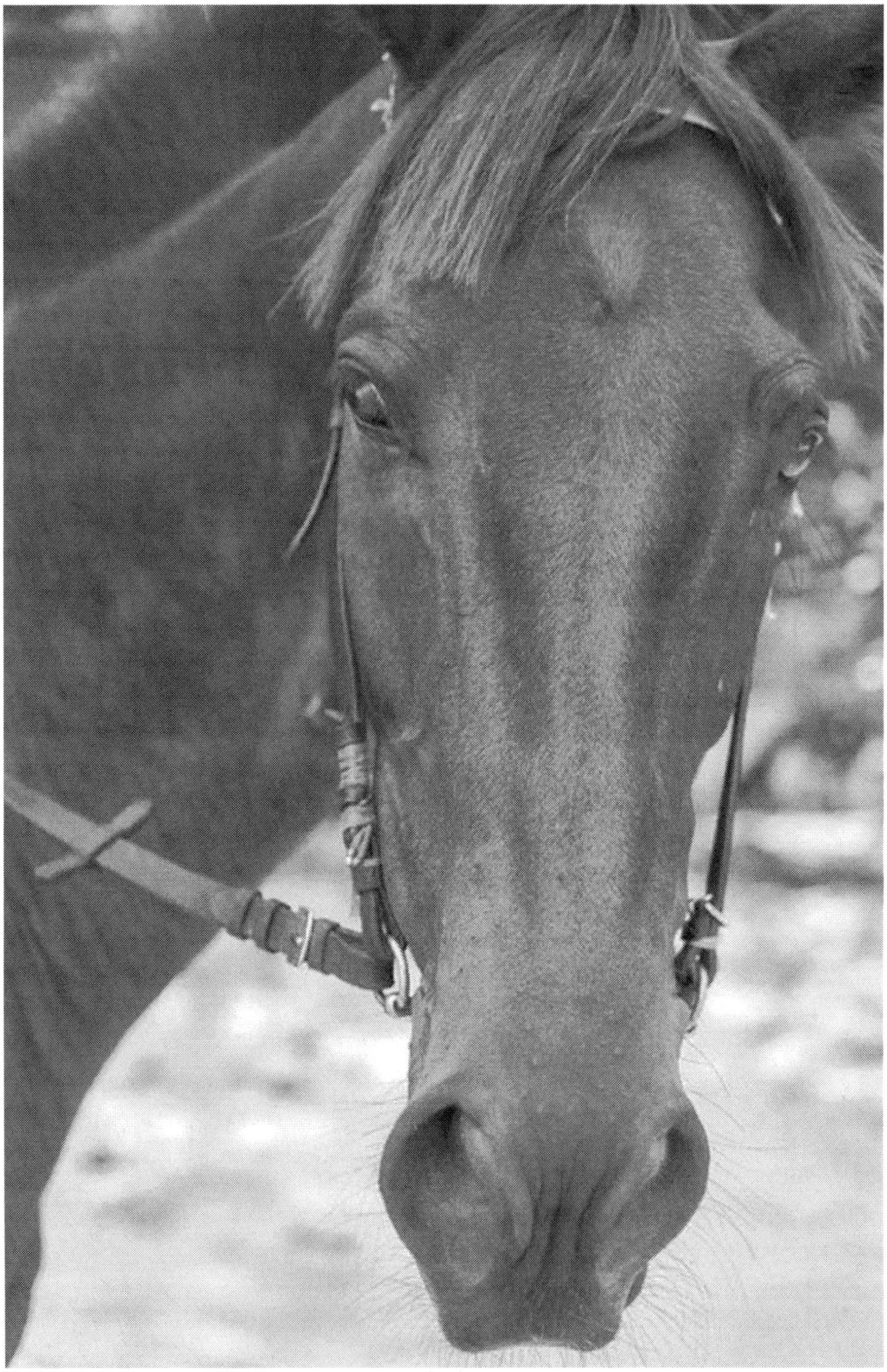

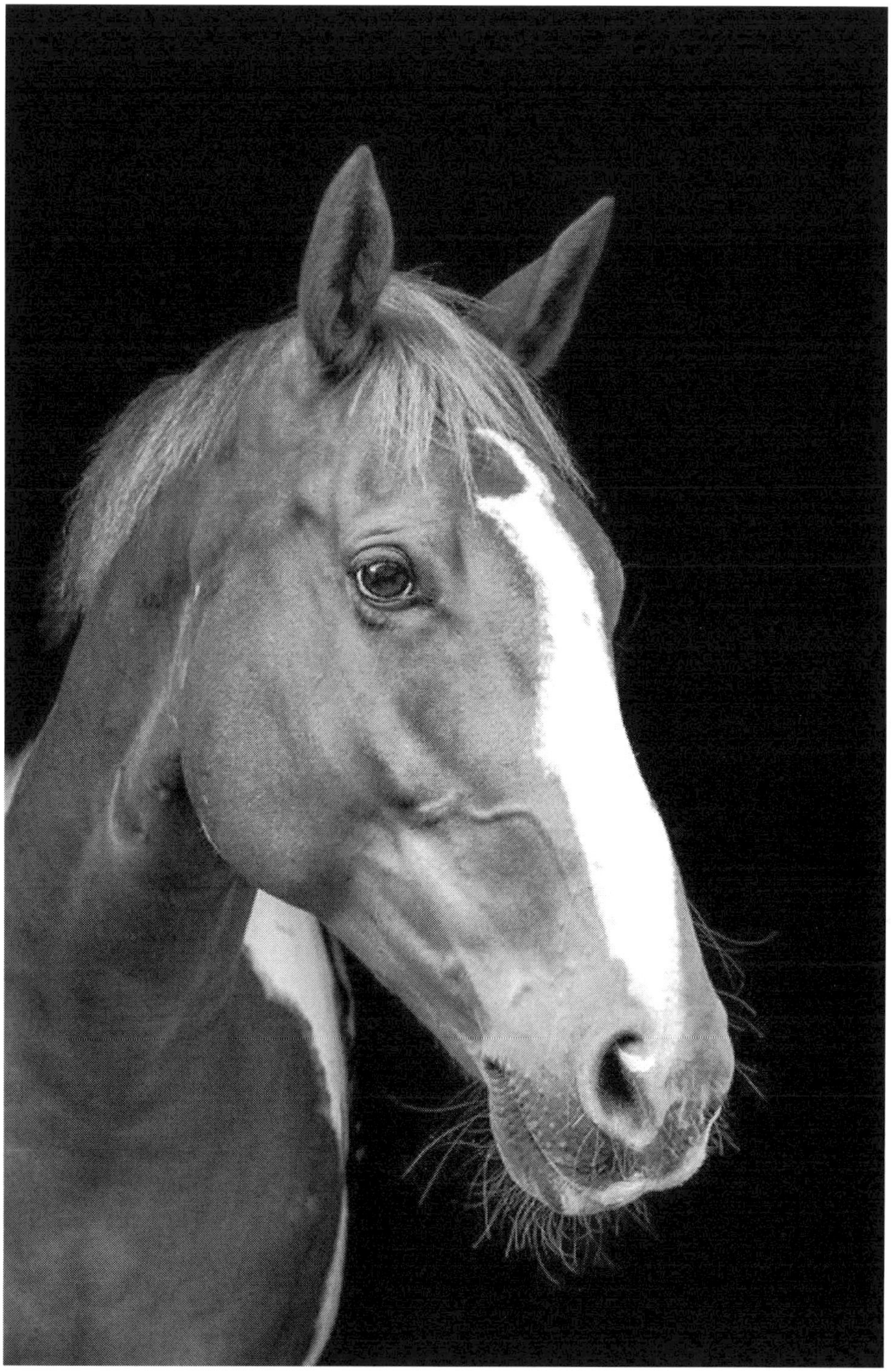

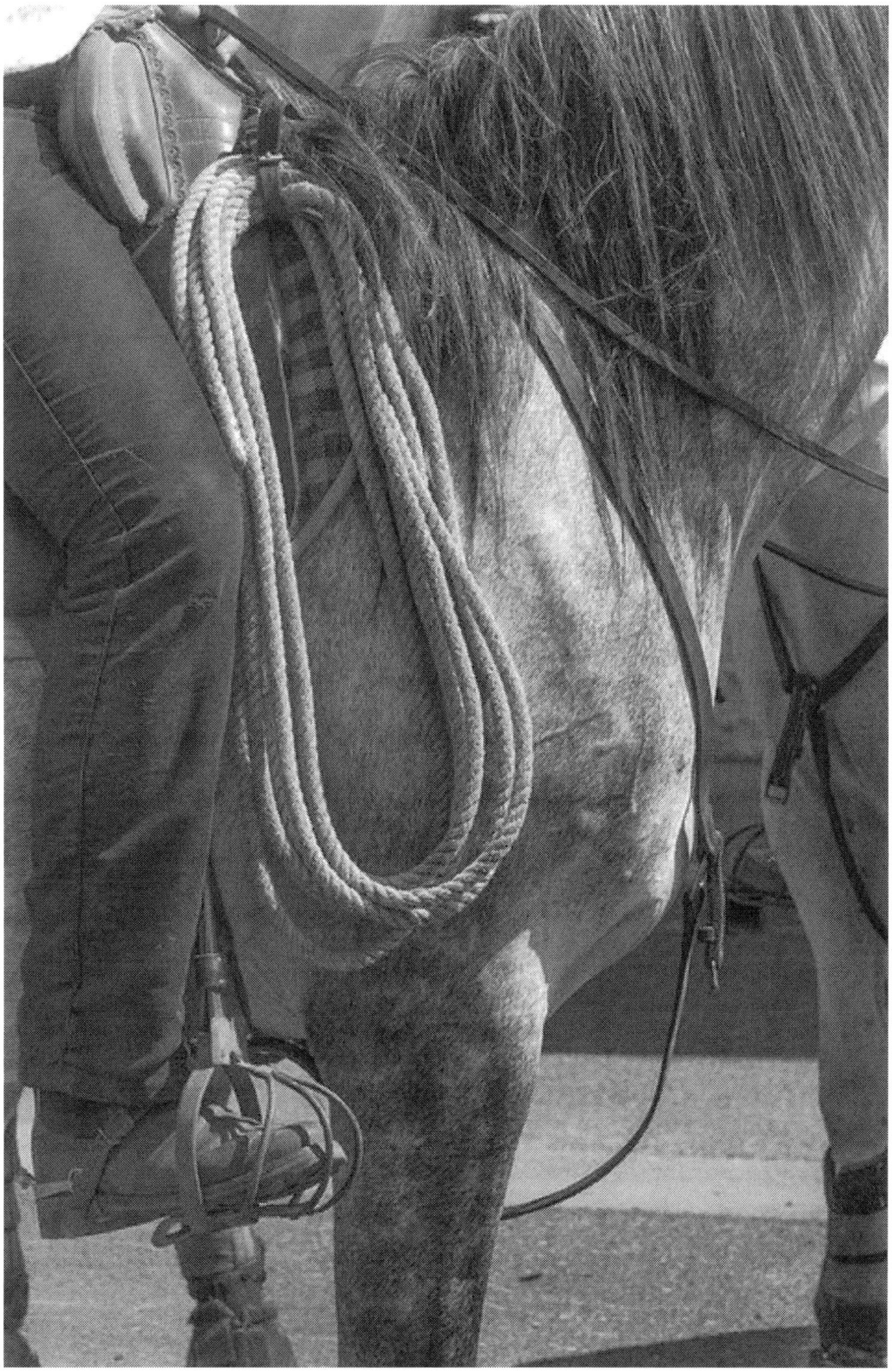

002

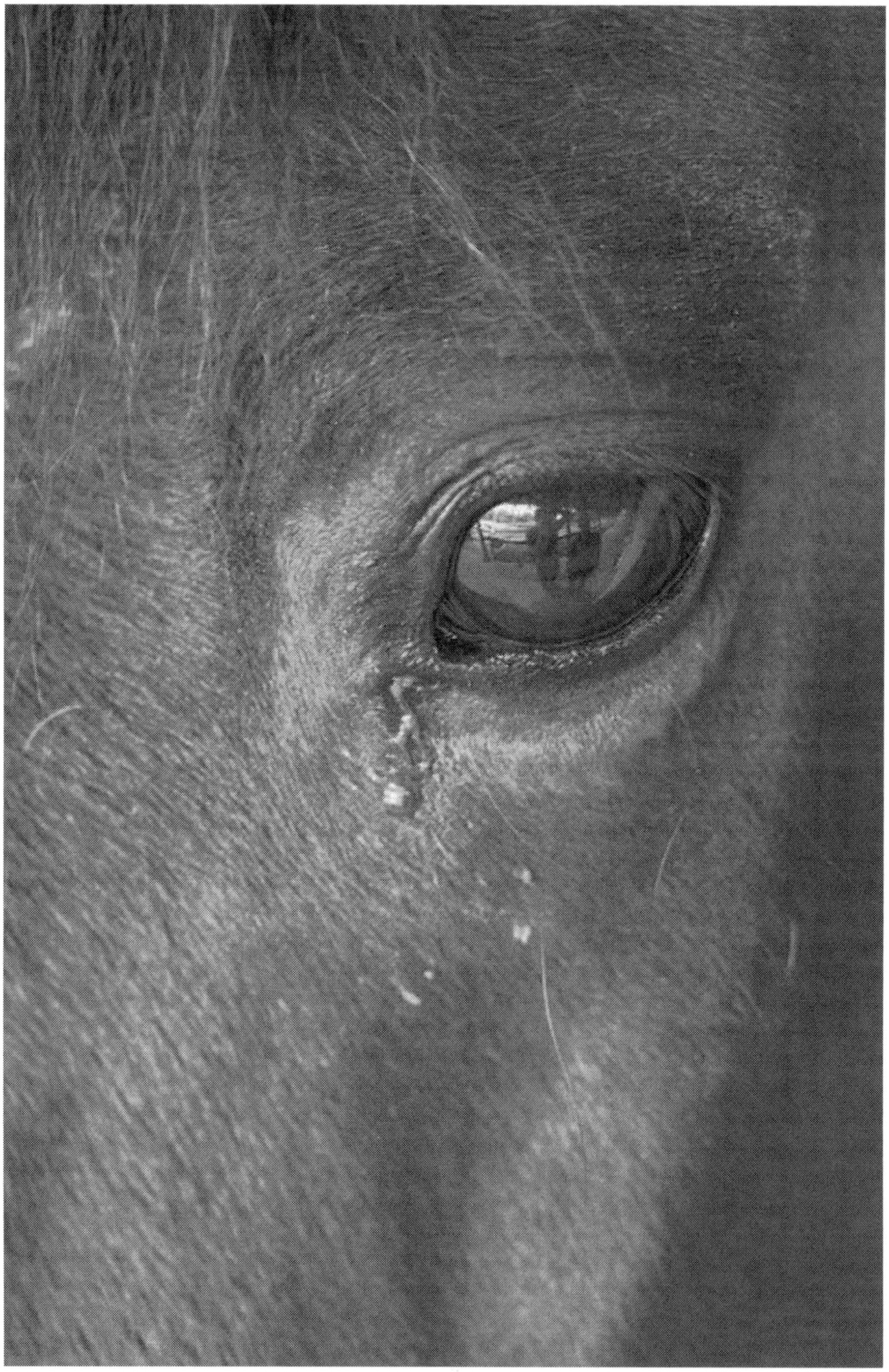

11
4

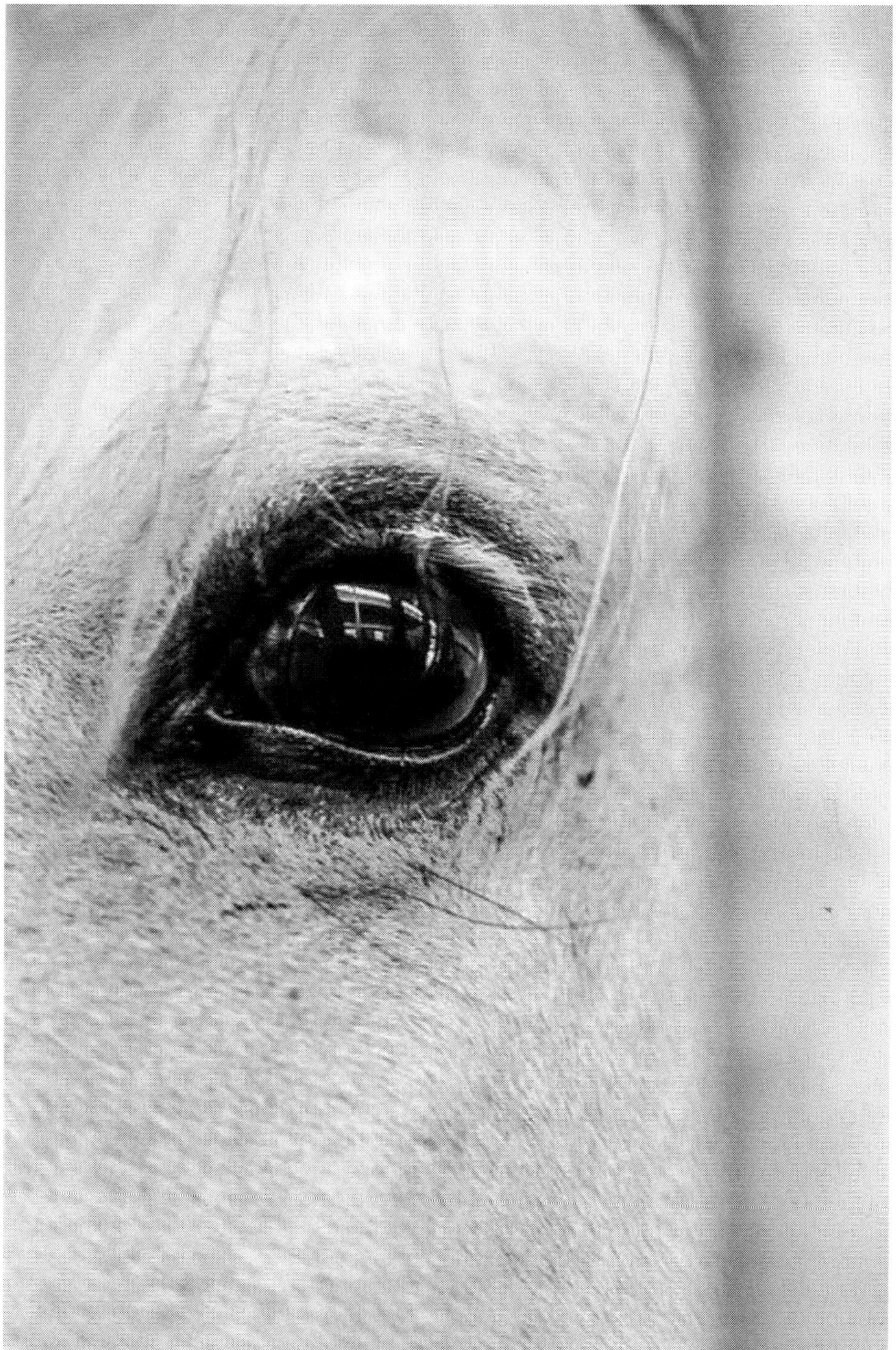

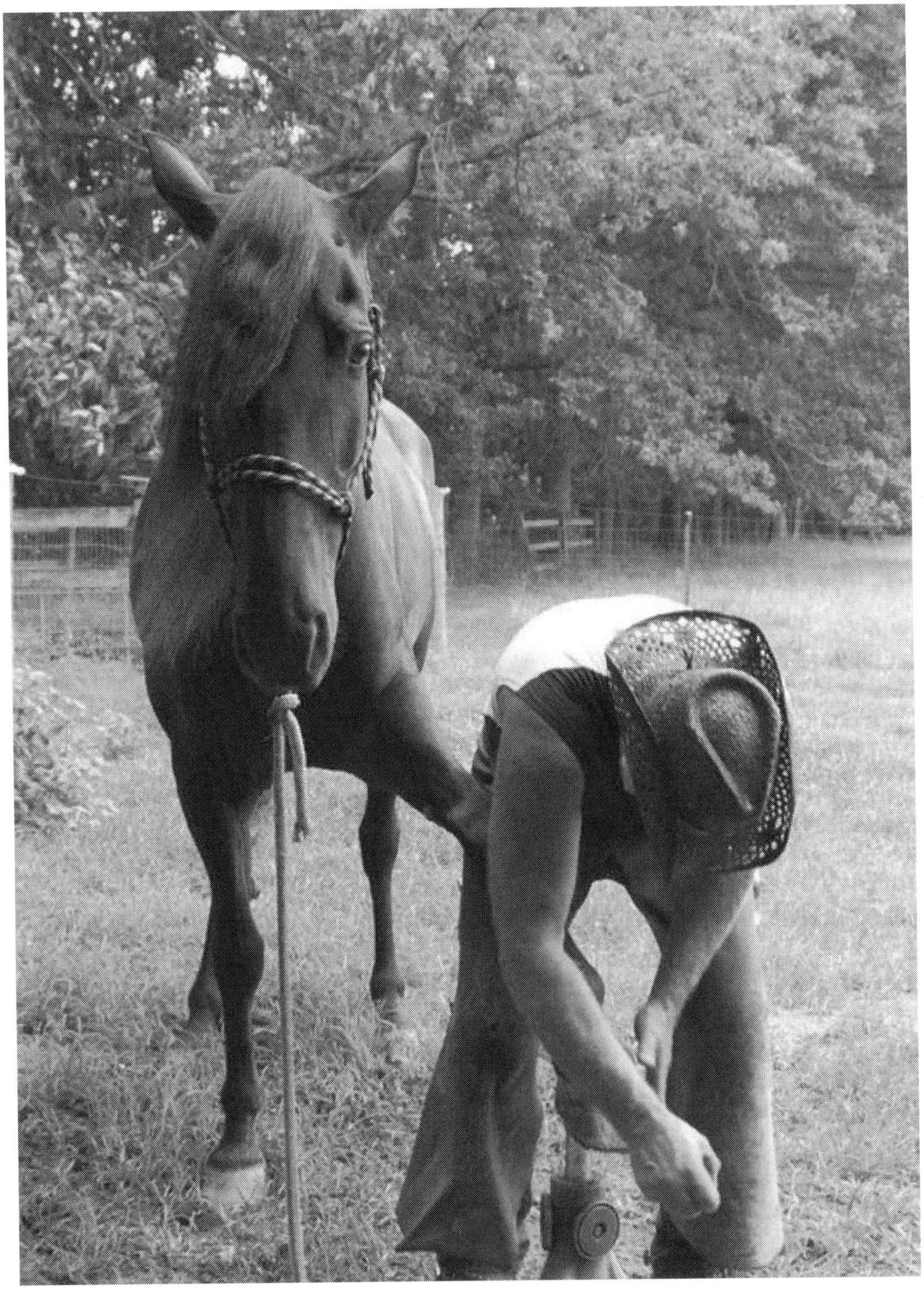

Wenphotos

The End

25607066R00060

Printed in Great Britain
by Amazon